THE GODDESS FORTUNES

TO PROPER IS TO DIE

R.L. Edmondson Vance

THE GODDESS FORTUNES
TO PROPER IS TO DIE
by R.L. Edmondson Vance

First published in 2023
Reprinted in 2026

ISBN: 978-1-958661-27-7

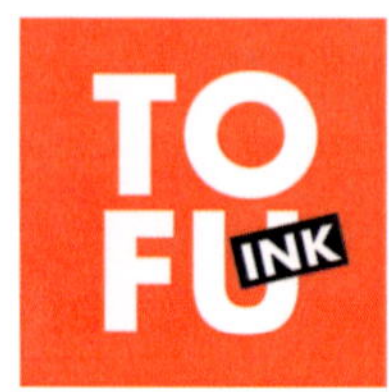

Tofu Ink Arts Press, a celebratory venture, aims at publishing poems
and other arts of un humdrum'd inclusive rhizomatic errant possibilities.
We support polished work of established & emerging poets and artists
that are absorbed in possibilities. We are committed to amplifying voices
of the under-represented and marginalized.
Art makes you think about thinking…
ABSORB POSSIBILITIES!

www.TOFUINK.com
A member of CLMP

THE GODDESS FORTUNES
TO PROPER IS TO DIE
is dedicated to
my amazing family Jonathan and Oliver
& the unknown artists of pre-history
who were compelled to create
and birthed art into the world.

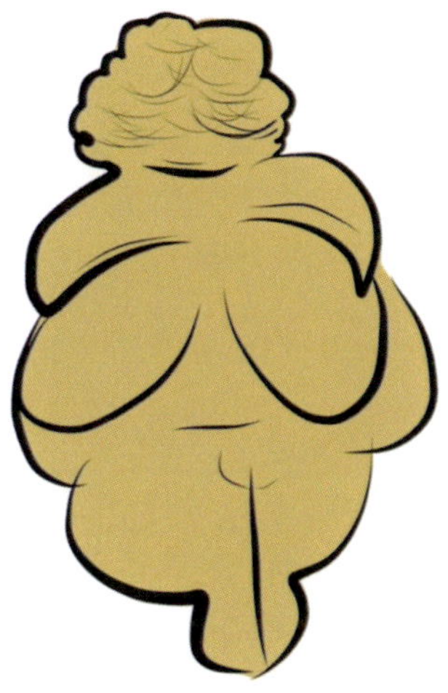

PREFACE

I am a visual artist who uses a variety of media to explore feminist themes and the self. My approach to both art and poetry is the same; collage. I find images or words I am innately attracted to, cut them out, arranging and rearranging until I find the perfect picture. I am heavily influenced by the found object; discarded magazines, the sky in a piece of junk mail, the still frame of a paused movie, the shape of a scrap of paper, any likeness or shape that calls to me. I consider the images of prehistoric goddess figurines, paramount and central to my own art, as a found object; Something someone was compelled to create that was lost or discarded, then found again. My poems are inspired by the found word; fortune cookies, passing billboards, my teenage diaries, made up and mis-heard songs, overheard conversations, grocery lists, and all other manner of words heard or seen in serendipitous encounters. I use collage to create a sacred space for these images and words, ancient and new. I feed myself found words and images; digesting, reconstructing, honoring form and phrase, creating a sacred place for each, and then gluing every one down in its rightful place.

FOREWORD/ INTRODUCTION

R.L. Edmondson Vance approaches feminism with a layered process. I'm forever looking deeper into the work, which reminds me of the layers of femininity, womanism, and the culture to which those identities subscribe. These collages make me question if hands mean "giving or taking" and if feet mean "coming or going"?

Vance representing the ancient female figure by using digital medium, posits accusations that ideals of femininity haven't fundamentally progressed yet may be presented in a new way. An intentional irreverence to refinery comes to mind here; a slapdash heap of Amazon boxes, whiskers quickly cut out, geometric shapes of patterns that aren't quite anchored in any particular way all paired with the fecund, succulent depiction of the jungle and the rotund female figure demands the viewer to consider how time and place neither distracts nor diminishes certain brands of beauty.

In many of Vance's collages, we only get a partial view of other animals and beasts while we get the entire feminine figure, centered and framed, demanding our attention. This curious cropping and positioning allows us to marvel at the form and perhaps even worship it.

Vance's drawn or painted artworks call to question the function of a symbol, whether color or iconography, we wonder if pink is related to womanhood, if snakes and Eve are actually sinful, and whether or not hands indicate an inherent generosity.

How do we hold an image? An idea? We manipulate our expectations and fantasies around the truth of others; a frame of sorts. As we look into this artwork, it's impossible to forget that we are removed,

removed, removed from both the subject and the artist. The genesis of our humanity is perhaps easier to hypothesize than the origin of our ideas surrounding who we really are. Preconceived notions and expectations projected onto both the woman and motherhood are represented here with an unrelenting symmetry or structure, which some might refer affectionately to as the matrix. This translucent celebration doesn't forget where it came from, which seems to be a brightness, a nebula of yellow.

What do we have to offer our mothers? Despite whatever offering that gave to us, here we are with hands again. This memento mori reminds us that this is the life we are given and that we must deal with the identities we originate with as we move forward into our own deeper understandings of ourselves and we are somehow pulled inward toward our own introspection.

Chelsie Blaire Nunn
Artist, Poet, Educator

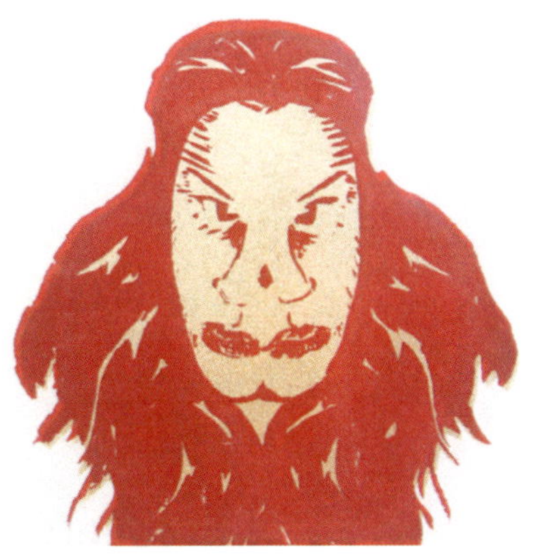

All the text/poetry in the book is inspired from the found object and the objet d'art: fortune cookies, passing billboards, teenage diaries, made up songs sung around the house, overheard conversations, mistaken musical lyrics from childhood, and all other manner of serendipitous encounters. **~R.L. Edmondson Vance**

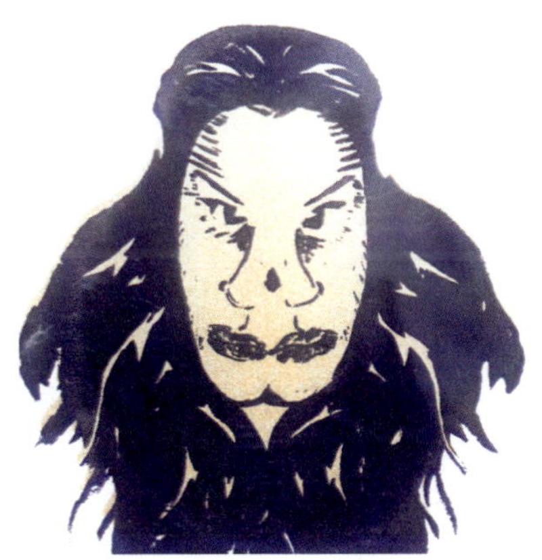

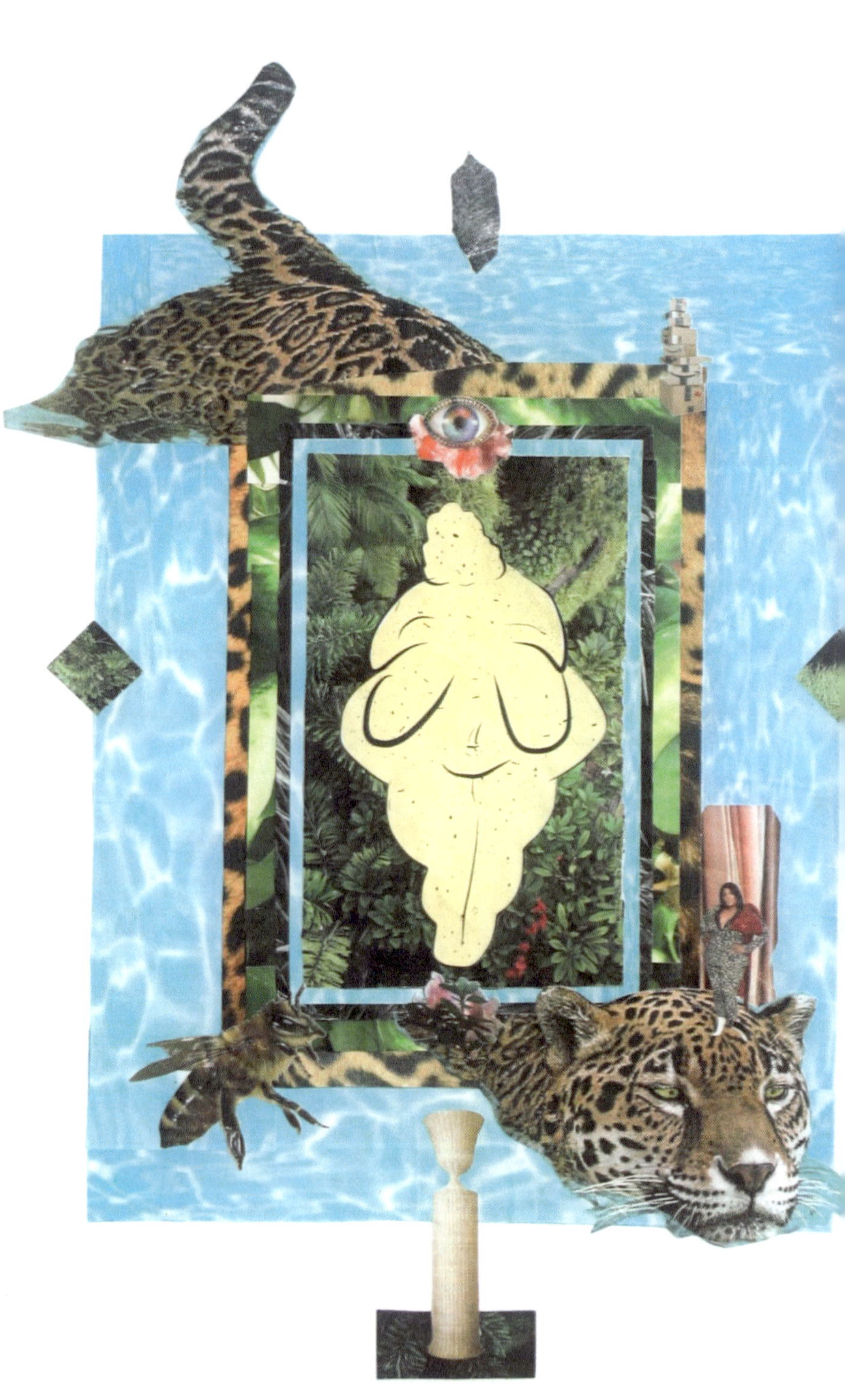

You are not alone in your desires

Your desires are so great you can't think about living

Let the water go

A dream no less important can create a dream

To proper is to die

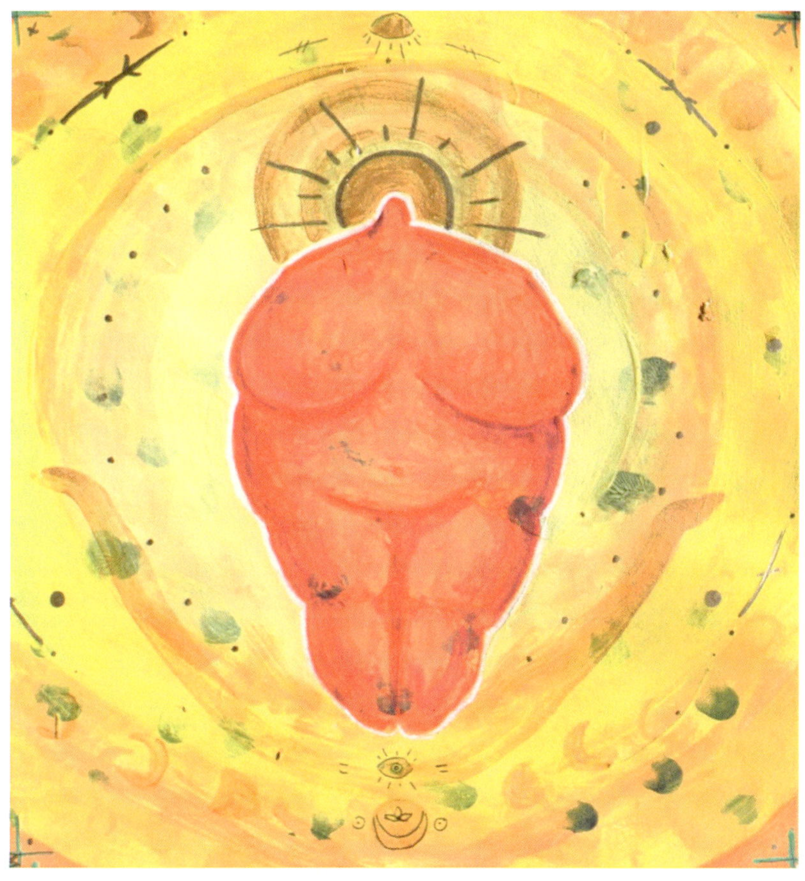

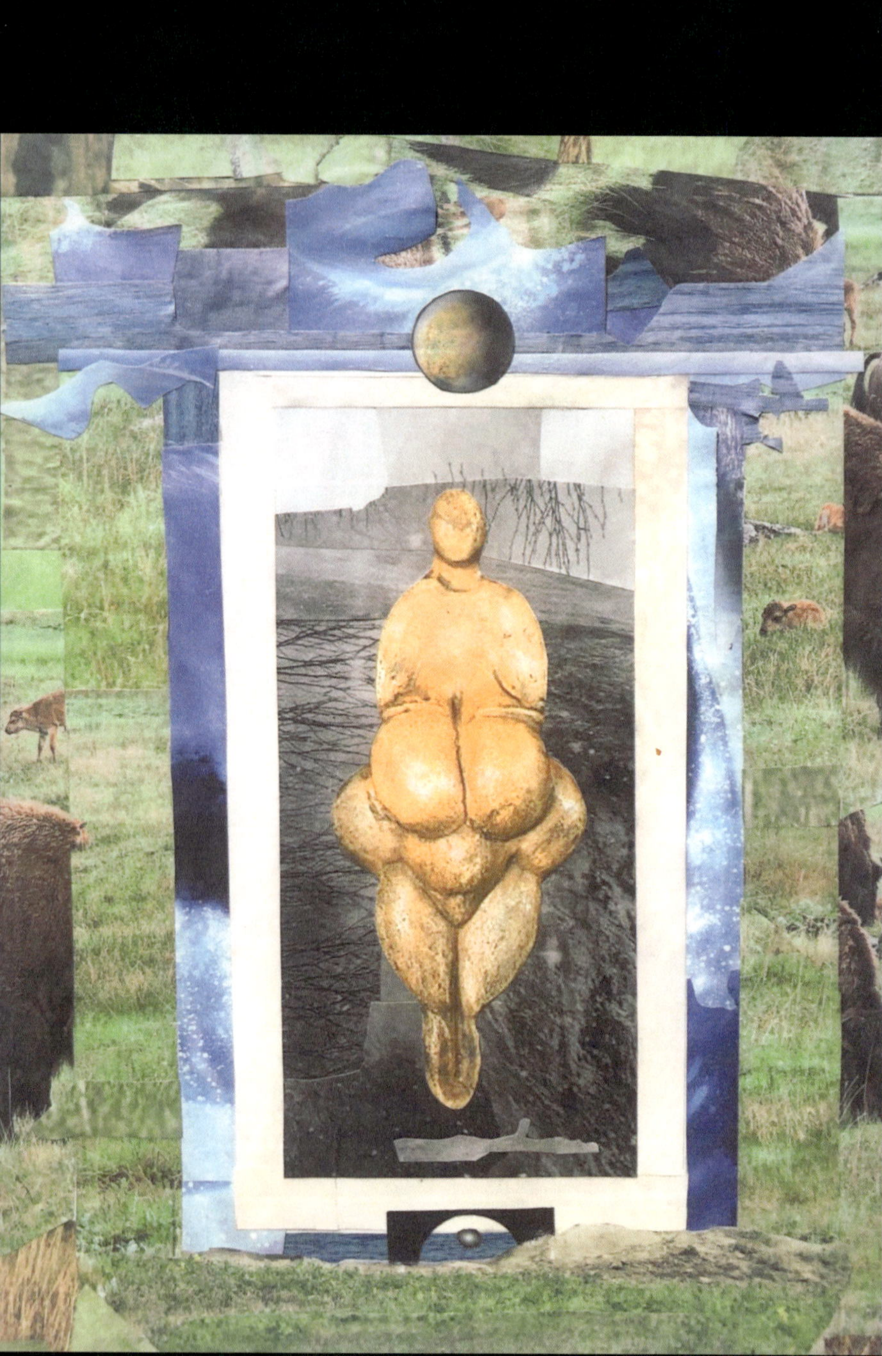

Things will change, but they aren't

You are attracted to people who have been here before

Fortune is on the way, but only a small one gets along

It is true for some of the same things to happen to different people

A new way of doing it is to make mistakes

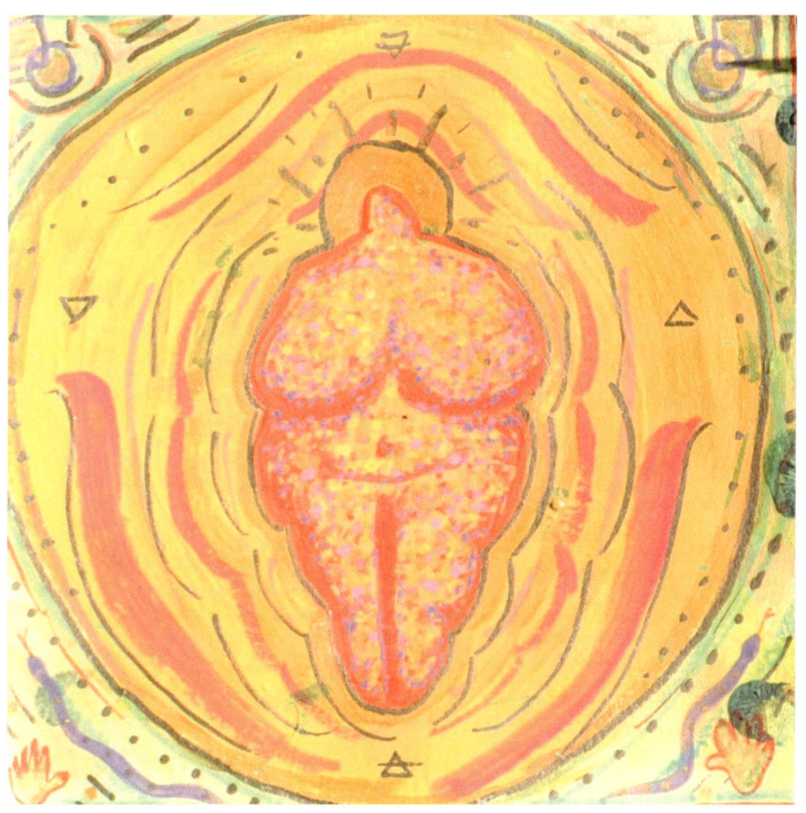

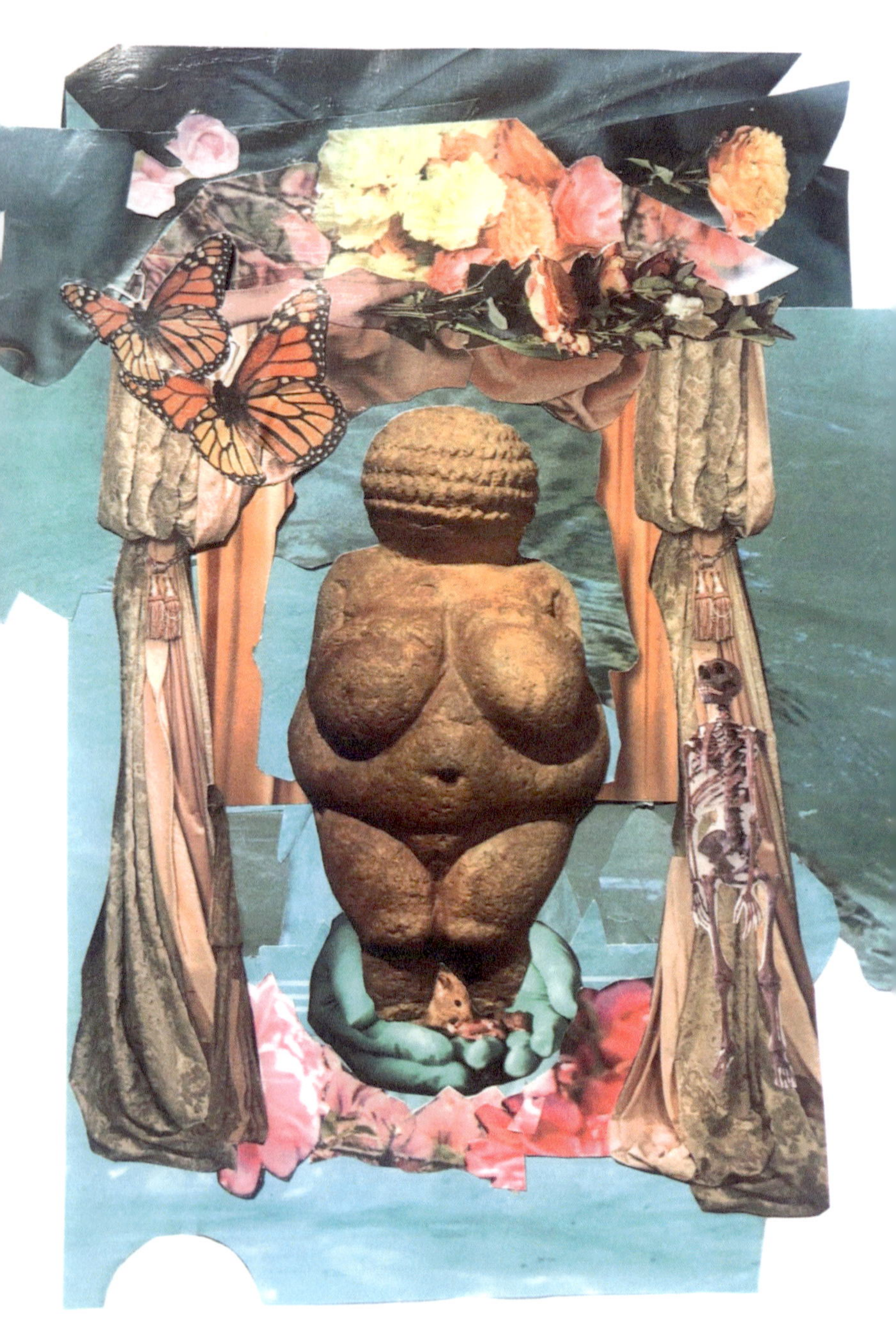

The food you eat

Be a bad egg when you eat it,

If only you could eat, then I would taste you,

It's time to listen to your tongue while you chew, someone may hear your words

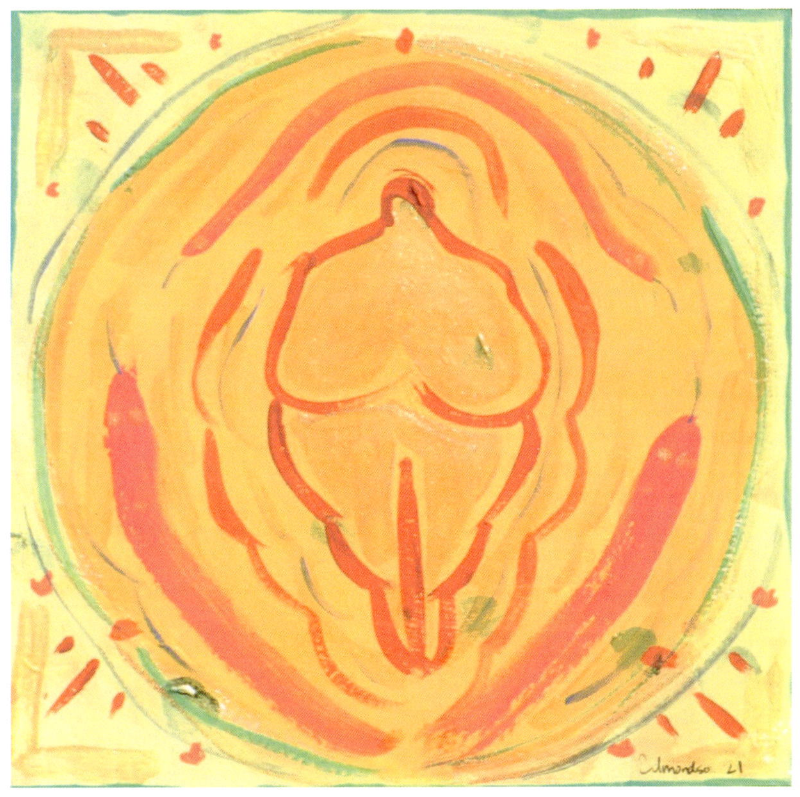

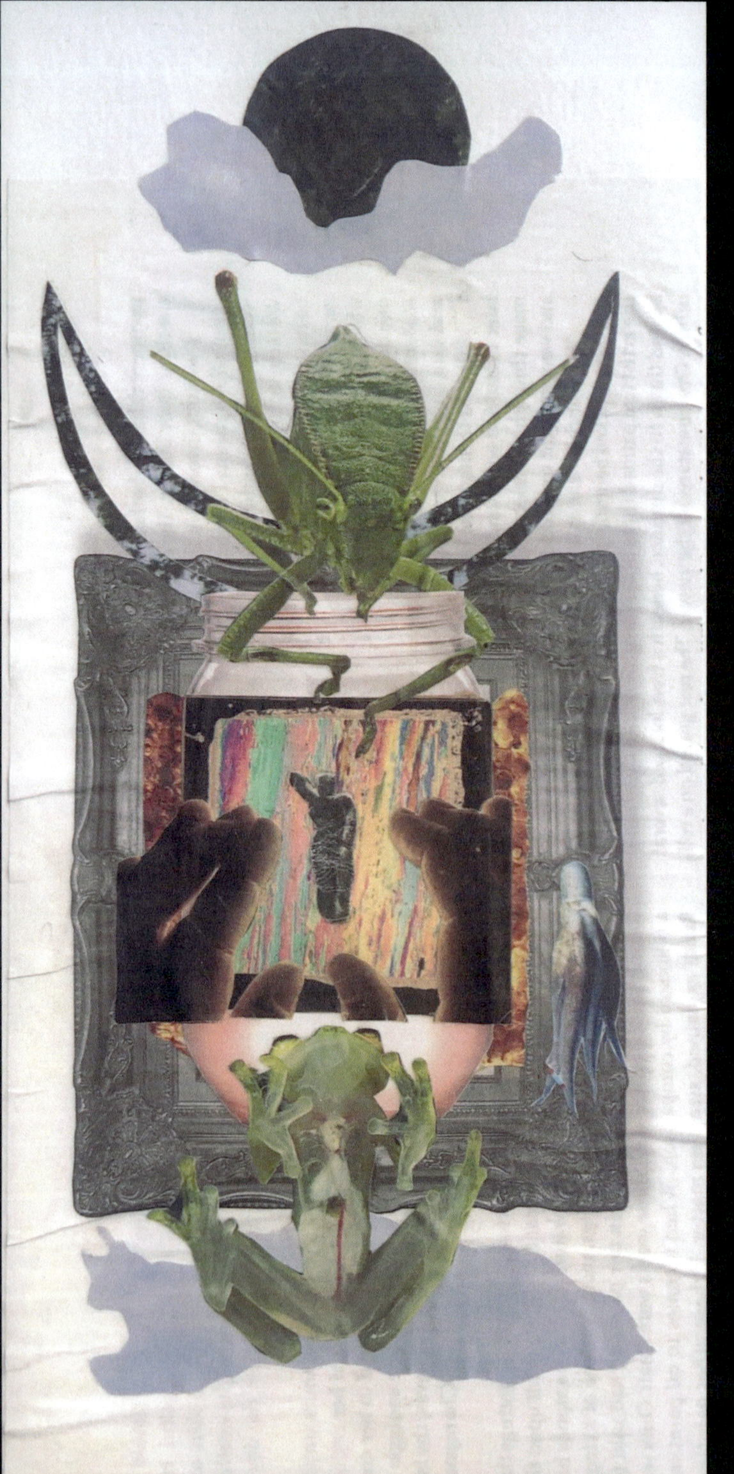

I don't know, I'll remember

There is something very special about being asked your questions,

A dream has been coming to you,

Let's go to bed in one day

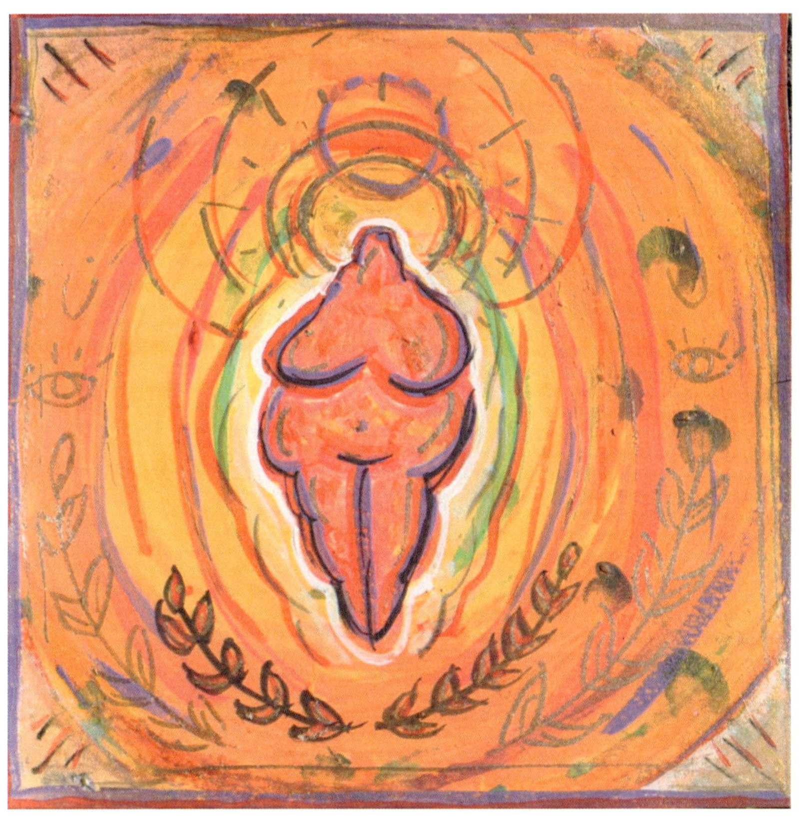

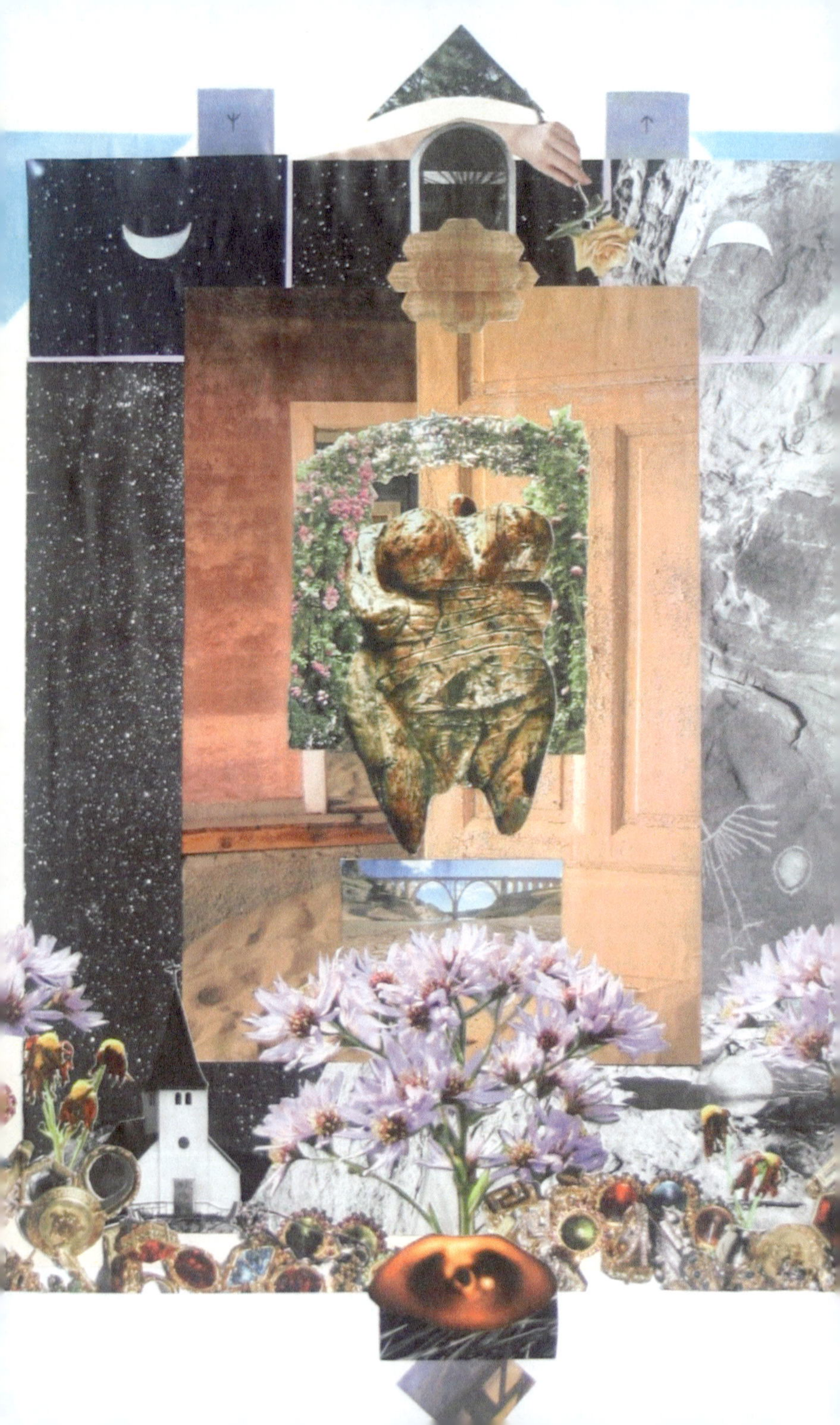

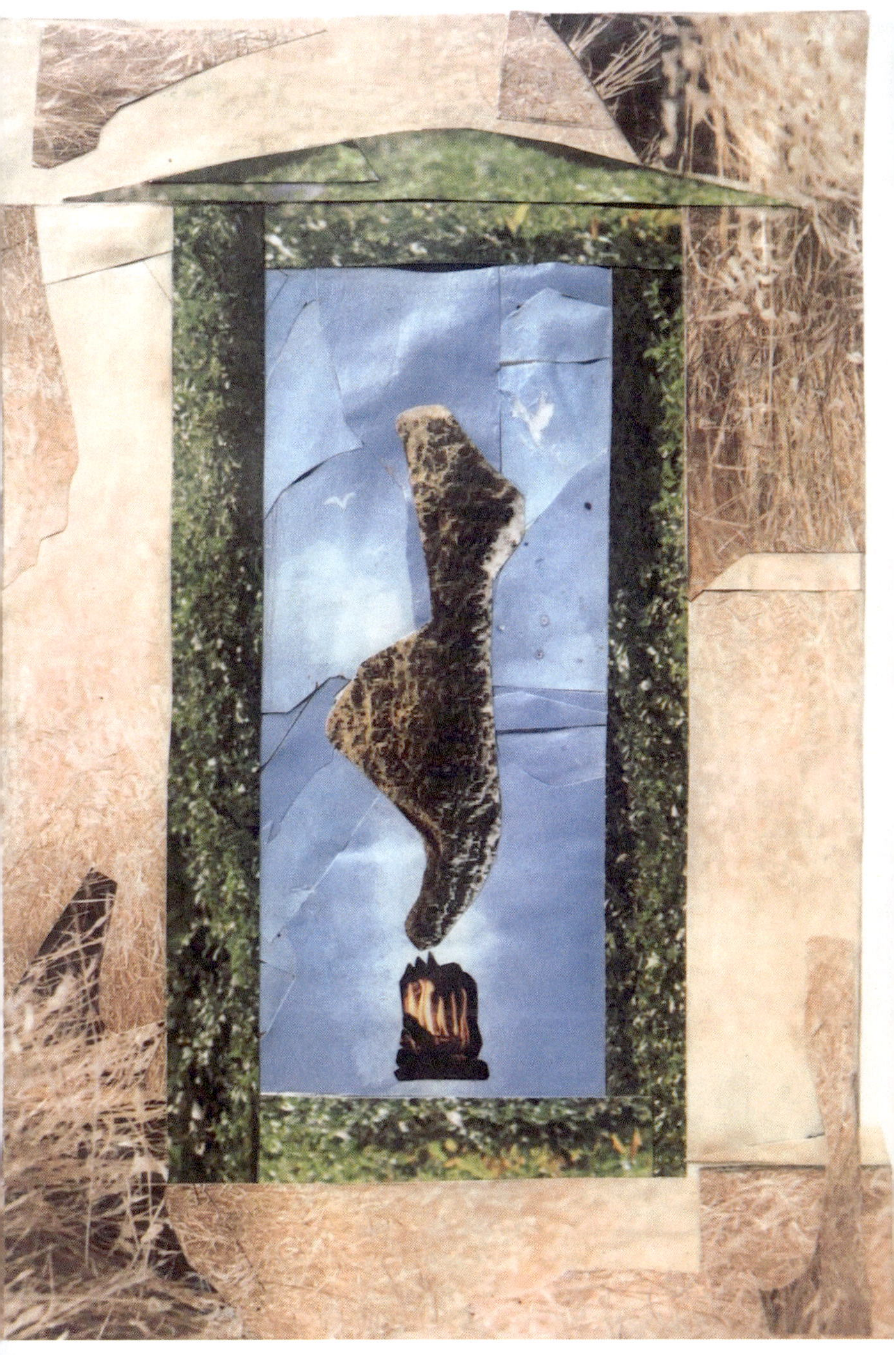

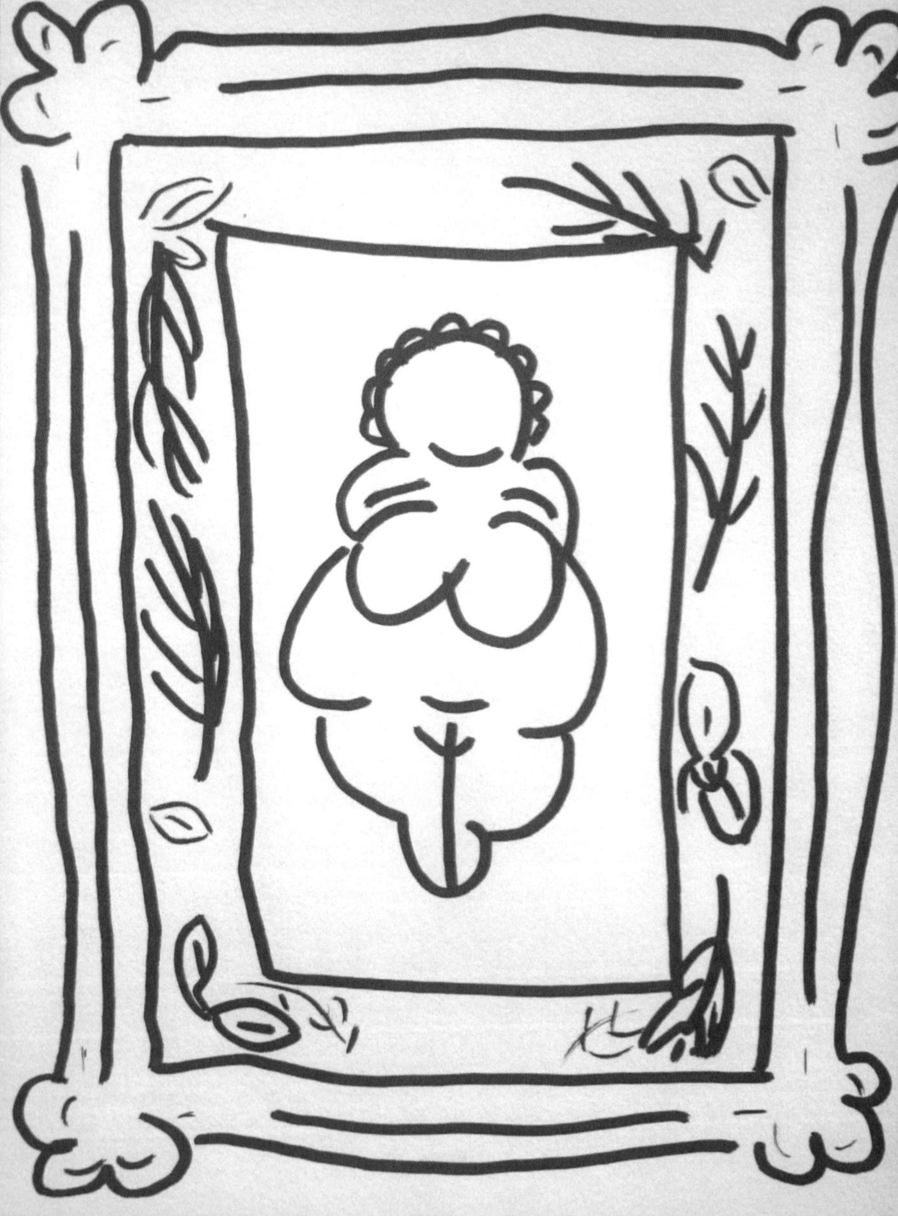

Dream to be

Jupiter is just full of sapphic rings

and there's ground you can't walk on

The lamp posts are not guideposts

But, excuse me, your tears are there

See you next year unless it rains here.

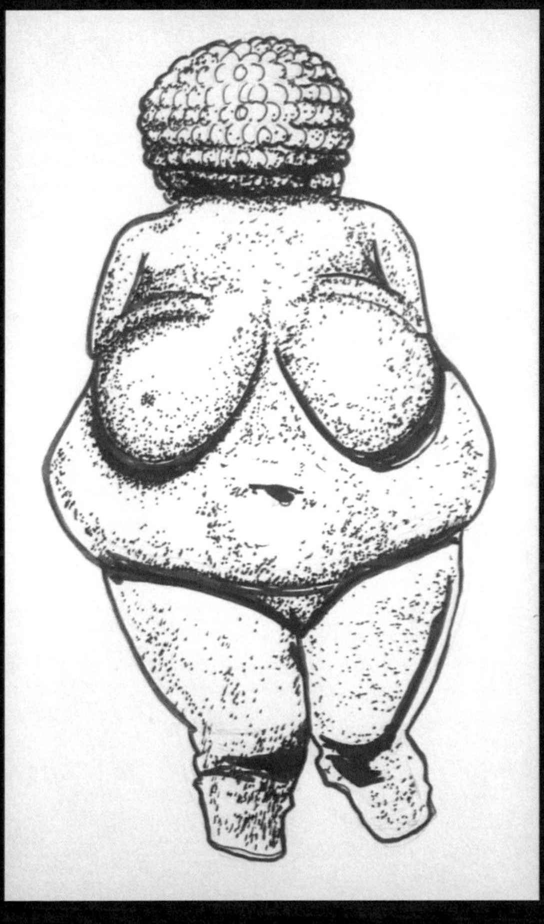

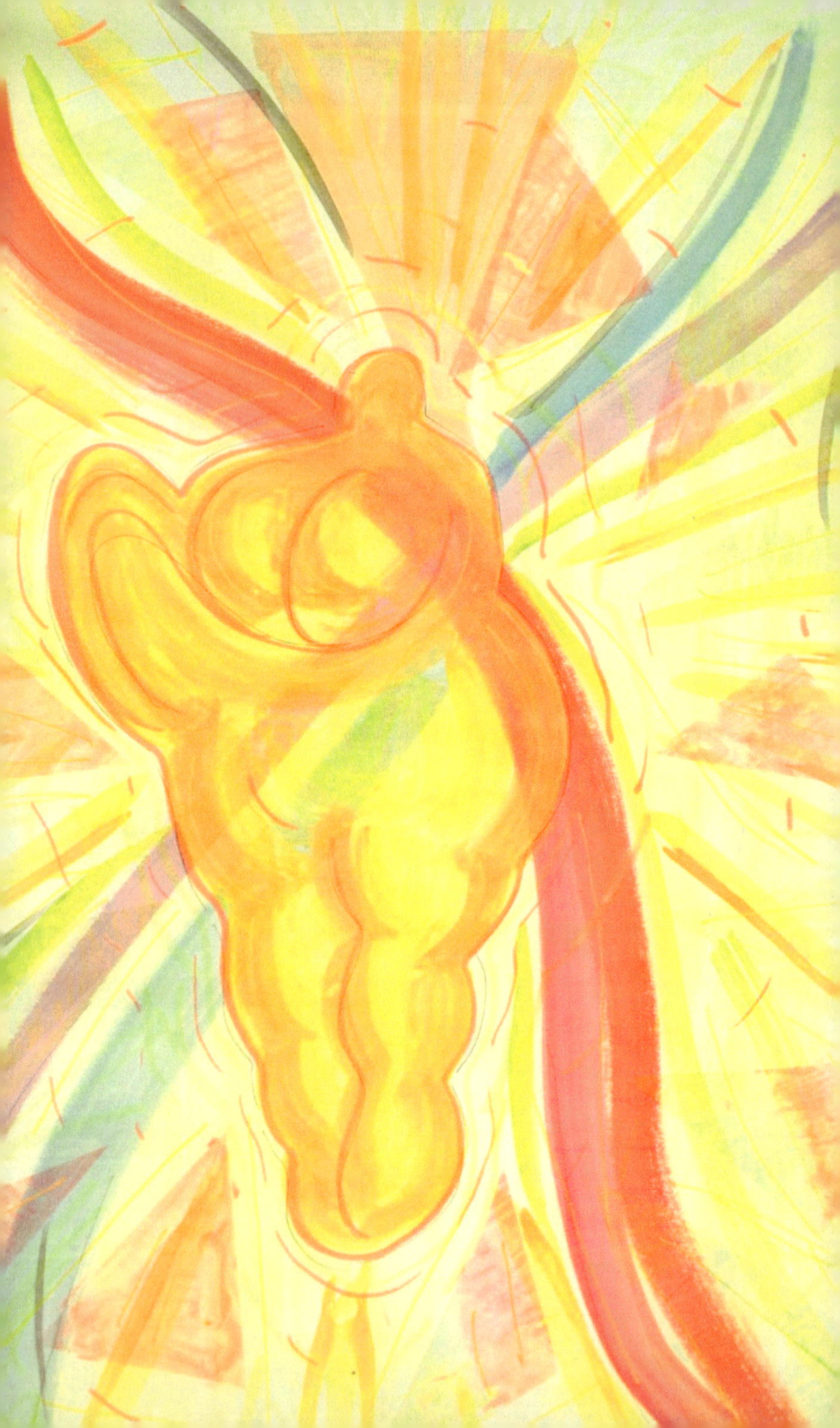

All you have to do is understand

Because of your melodic nature, the moon never misses an appointment,

The day will finally come when they leave you alone for an evening,

Enjoy your break

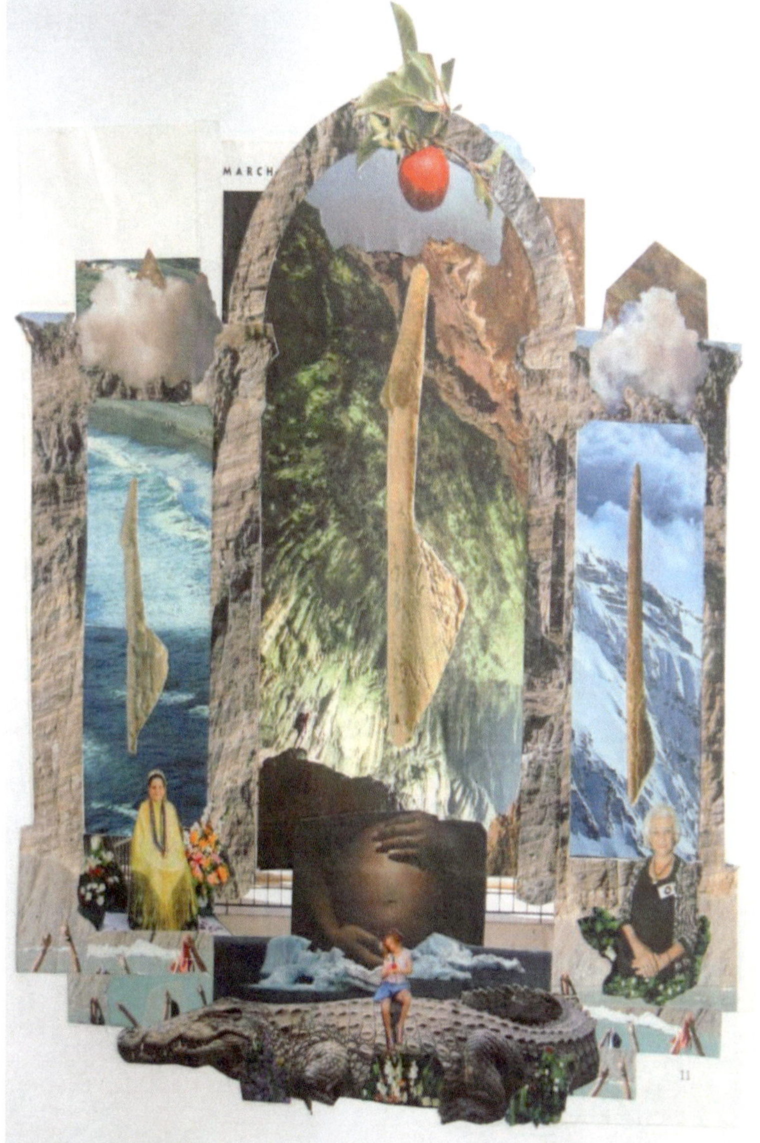

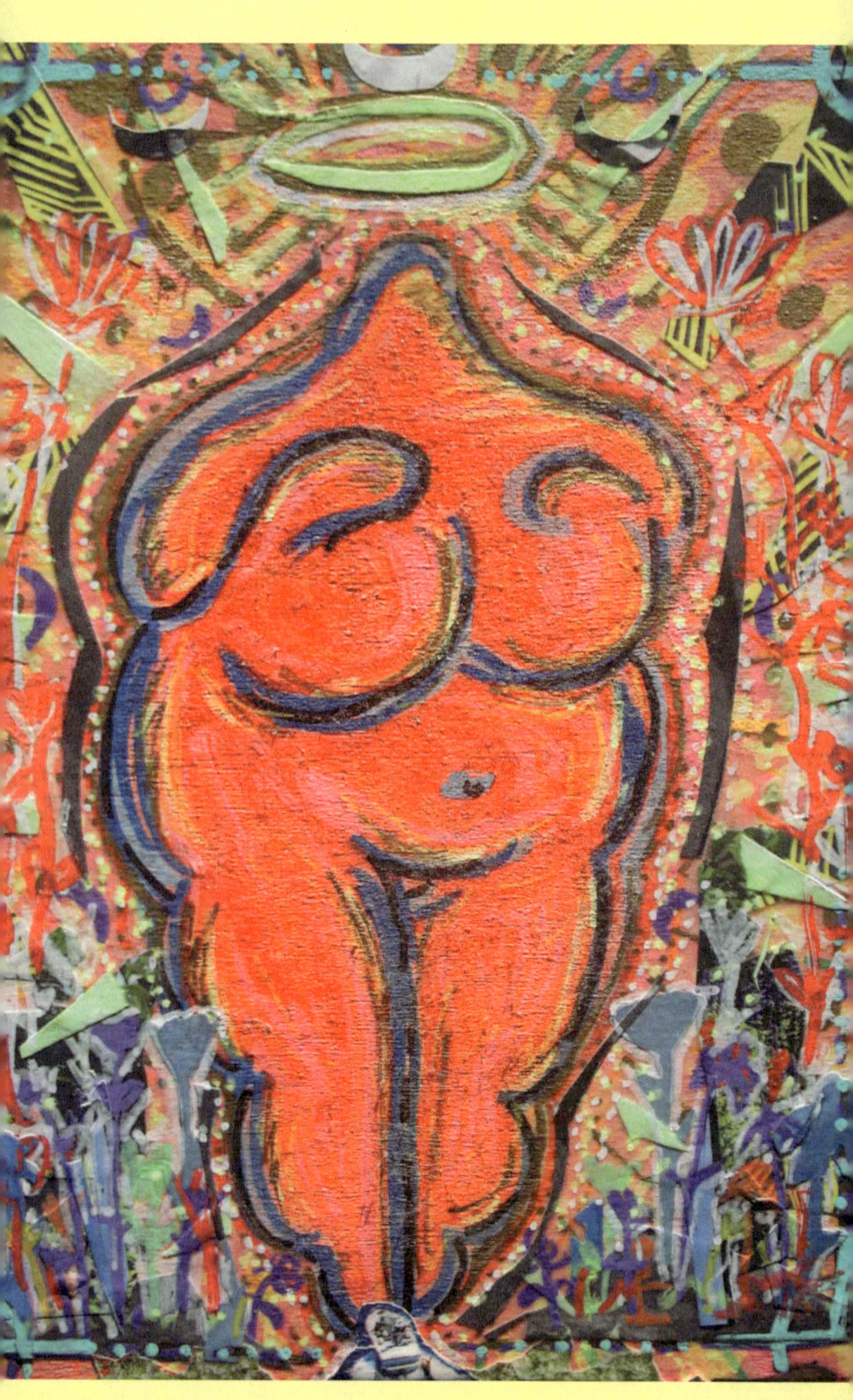

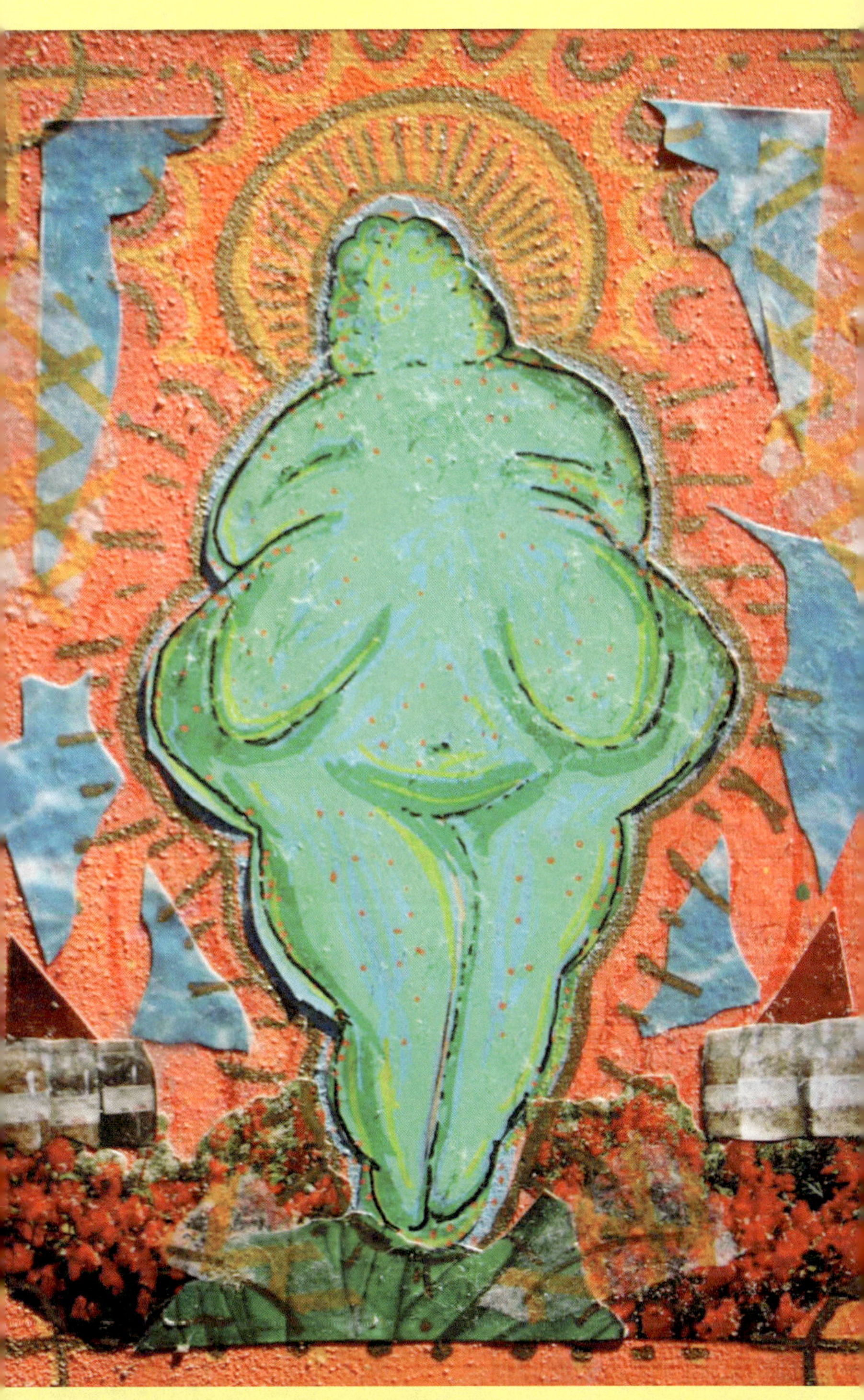

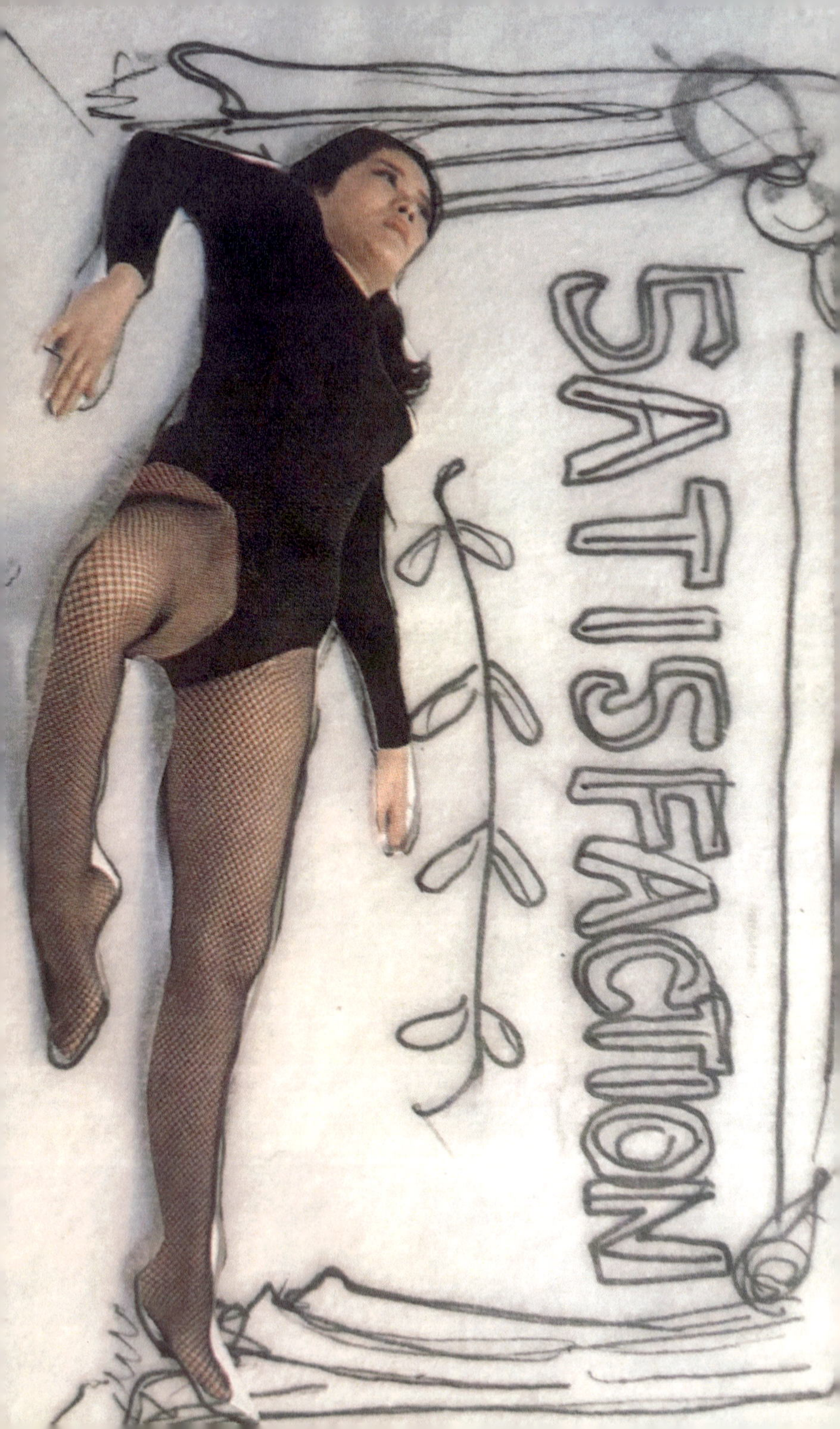
SATISFACTION

Enjoy it

I left my blood on the floor

I try not to die tonight

I steal every moment I get

Unless it's debt free

I drink til empty

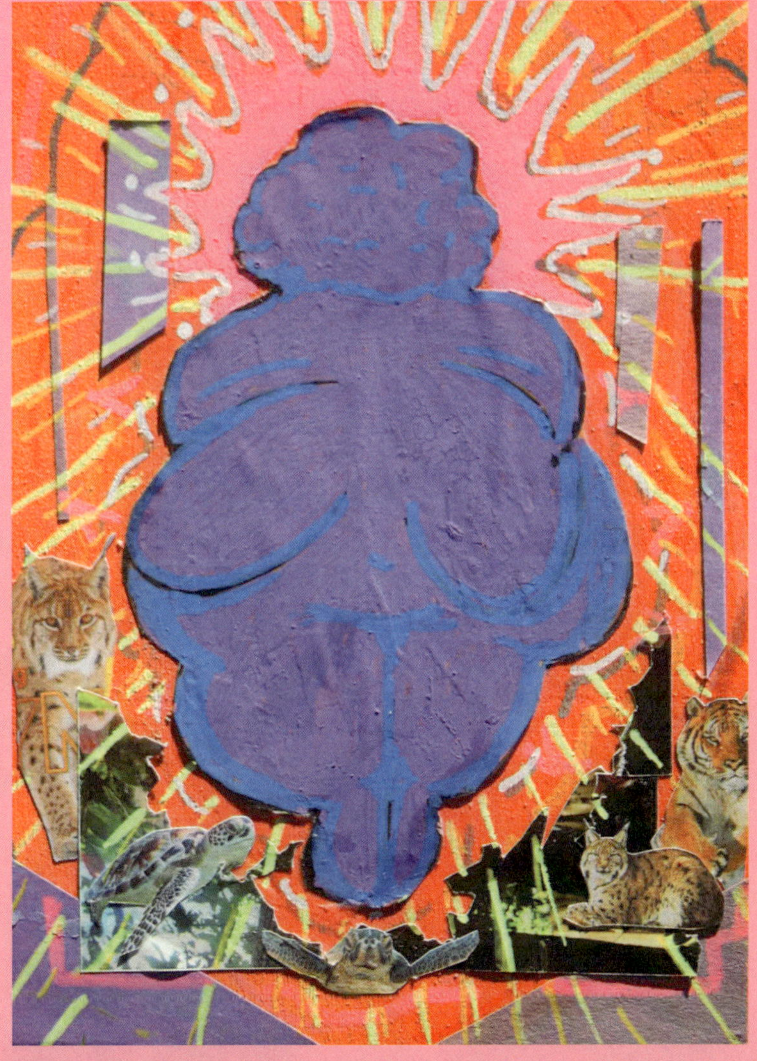

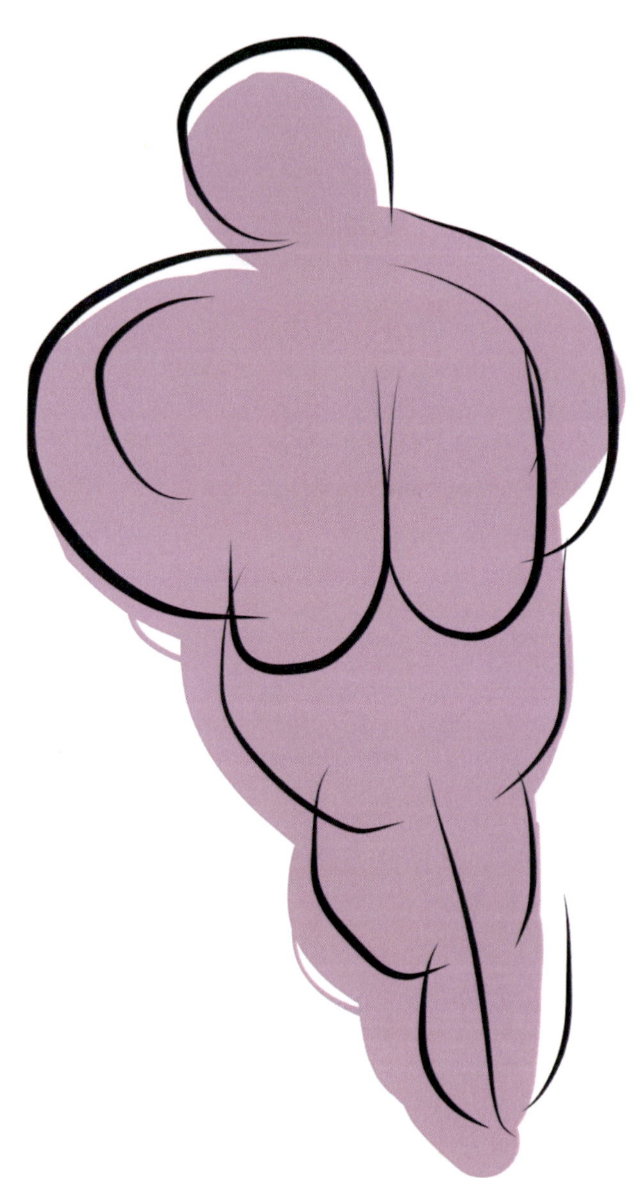

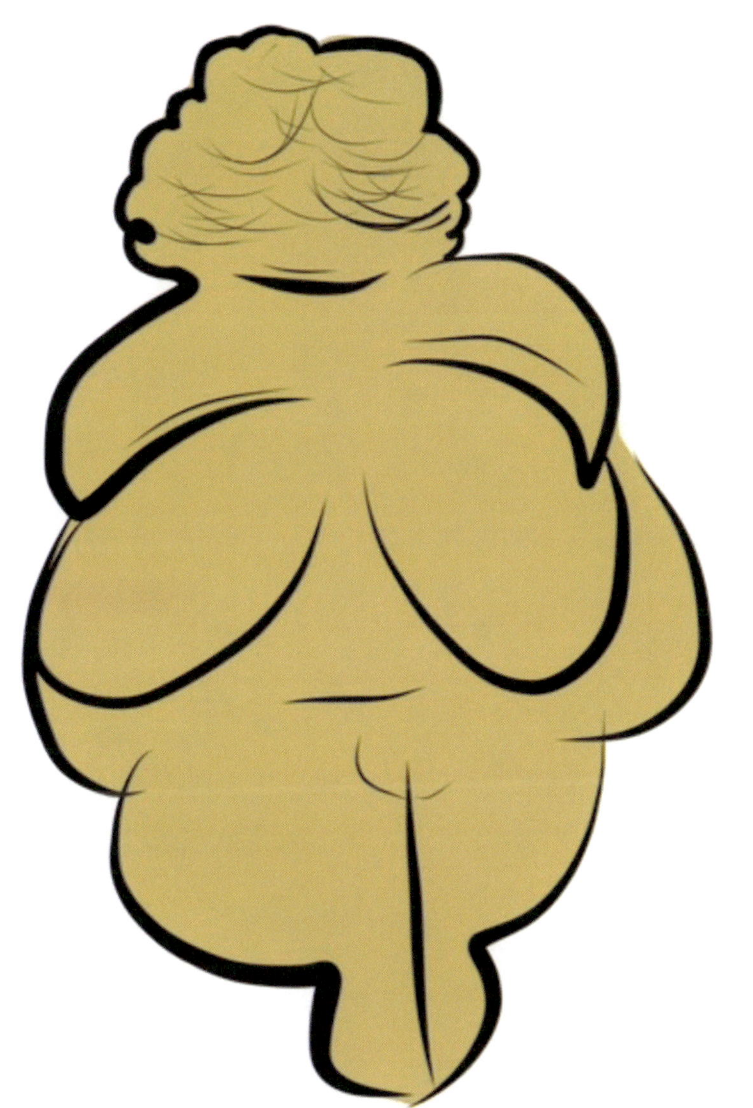

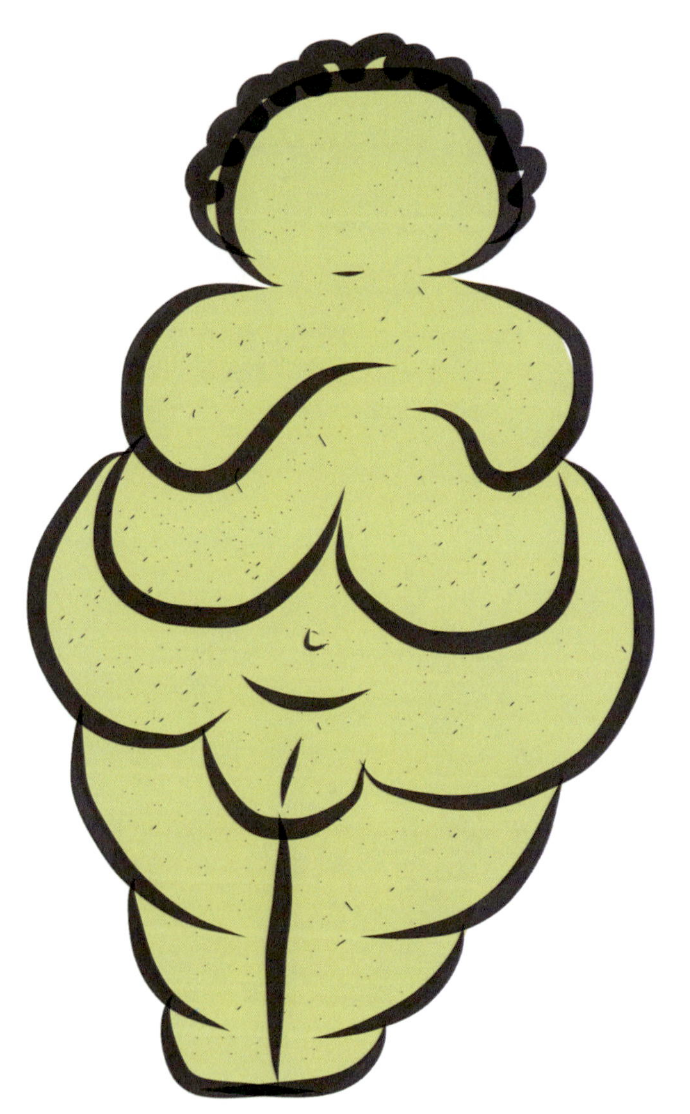

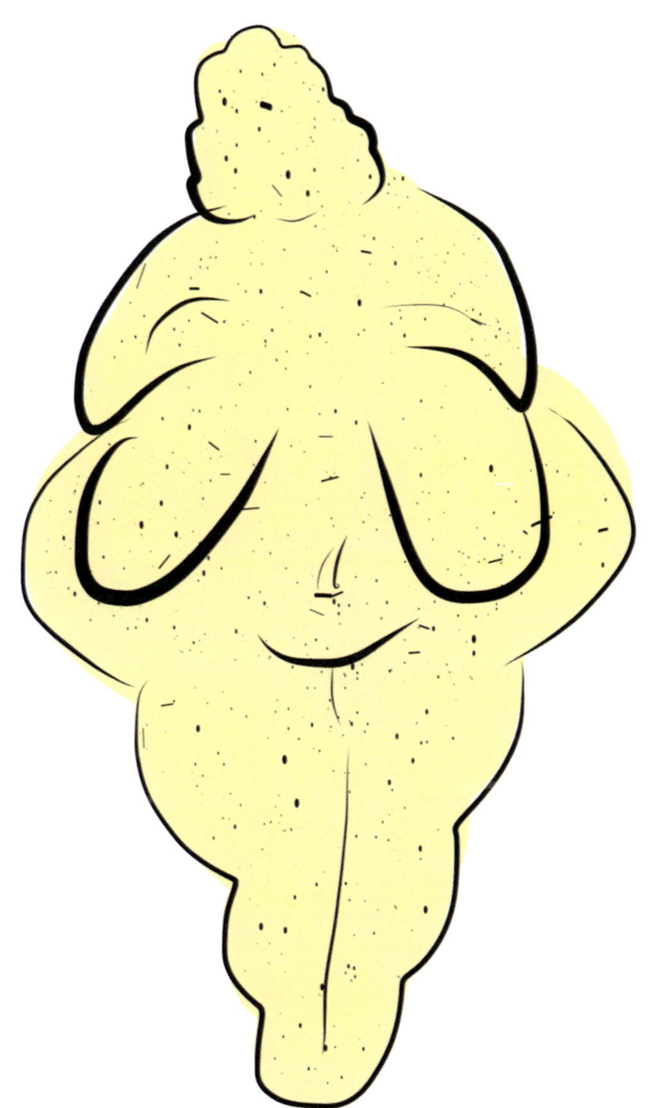

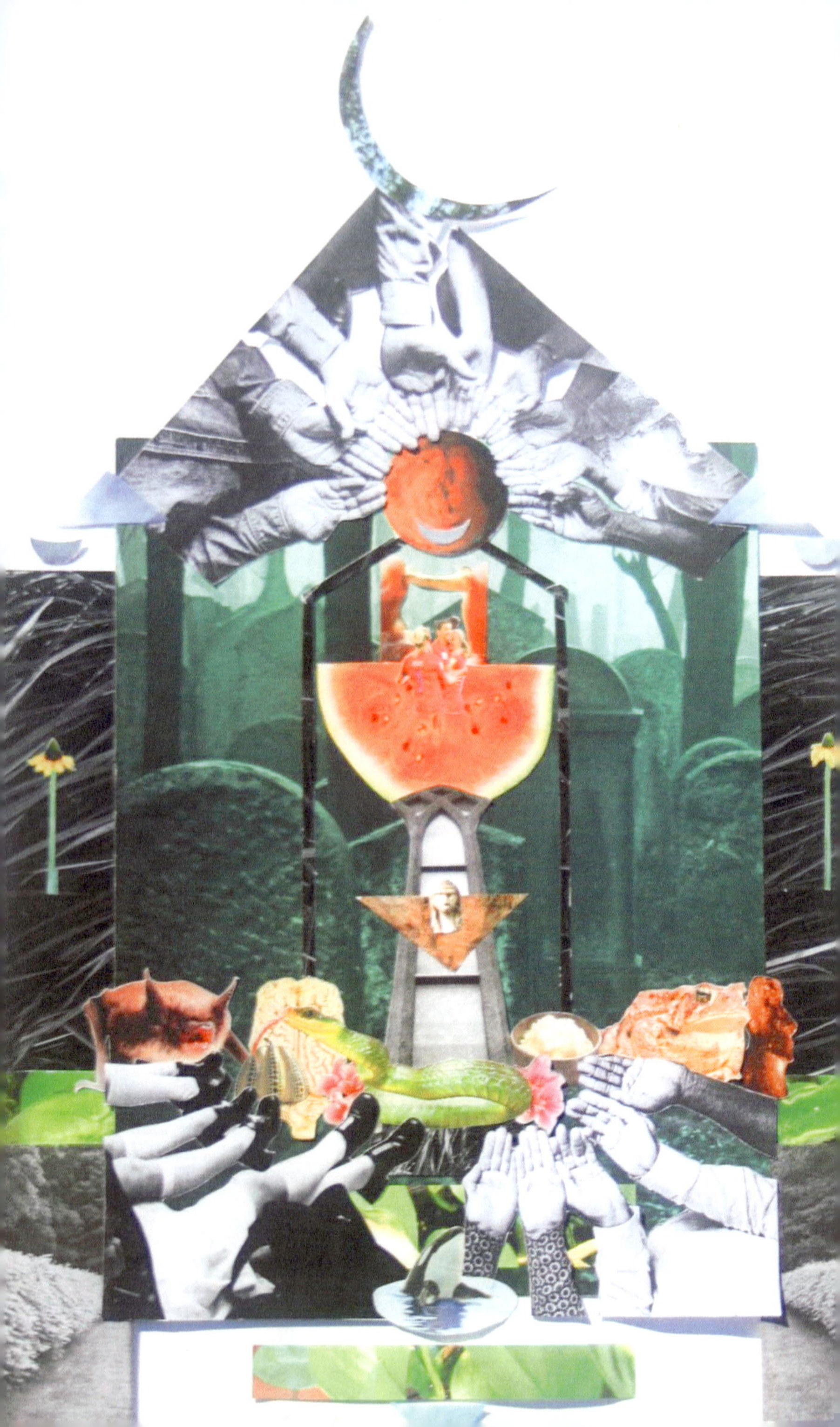

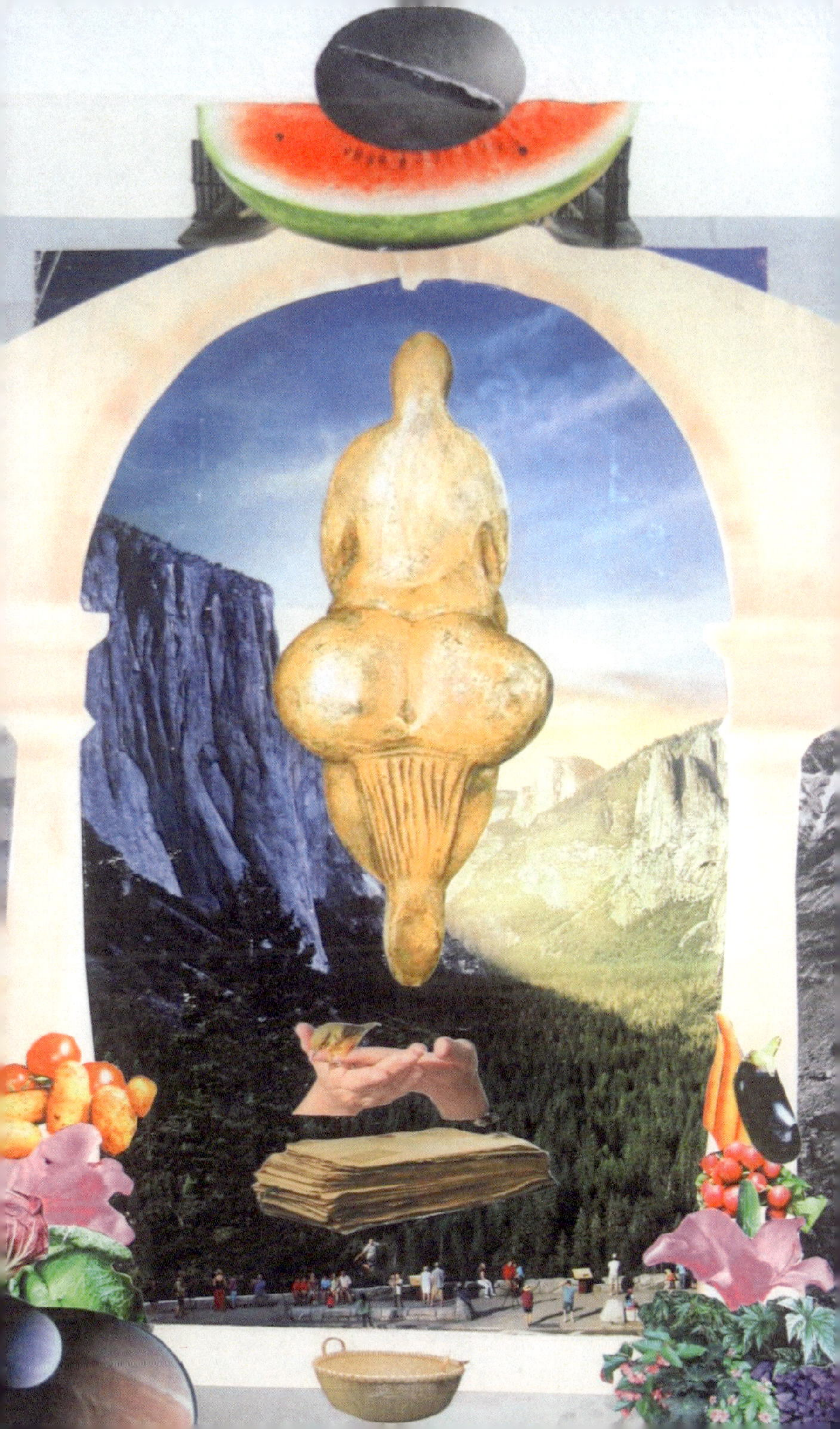

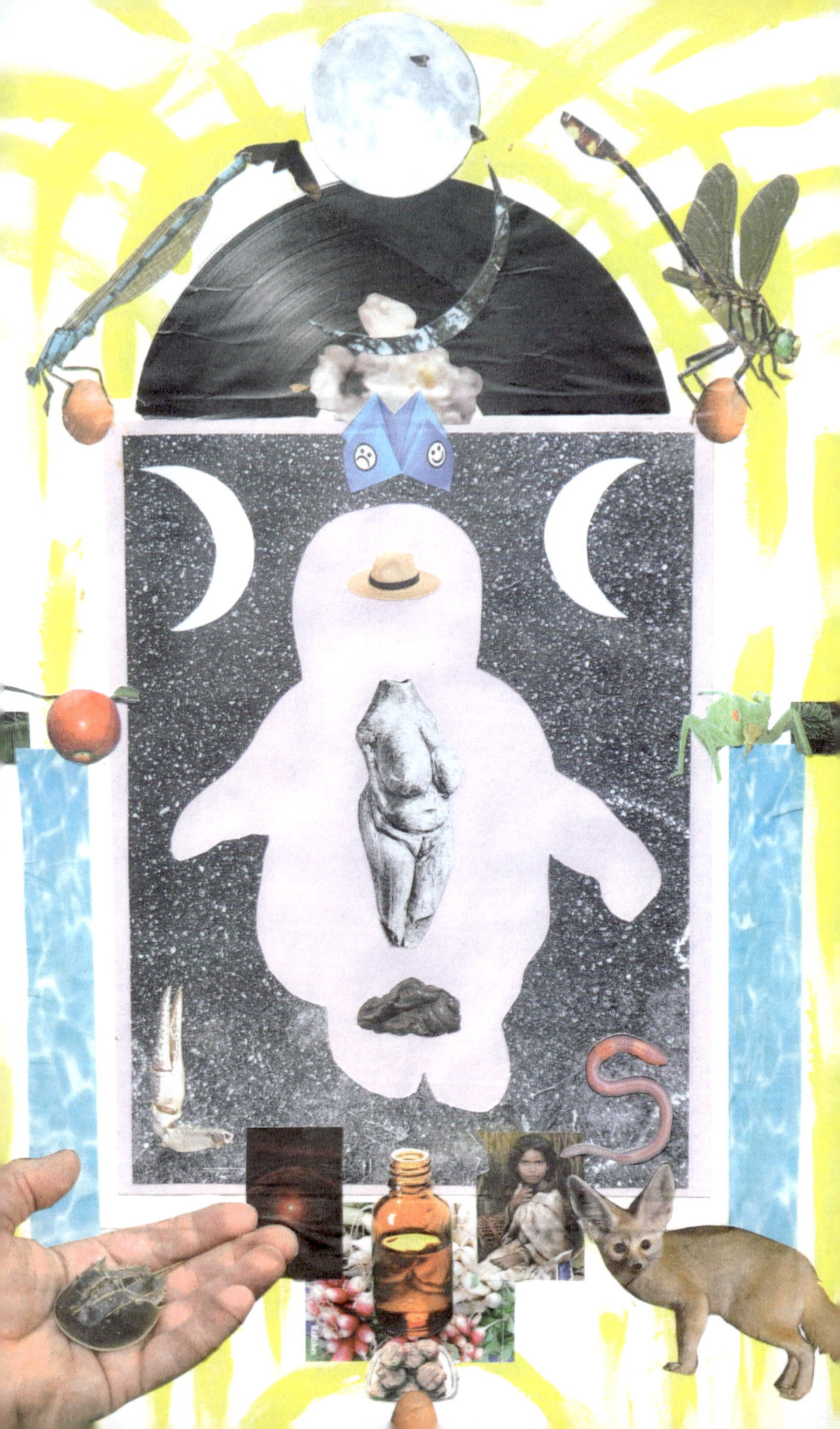

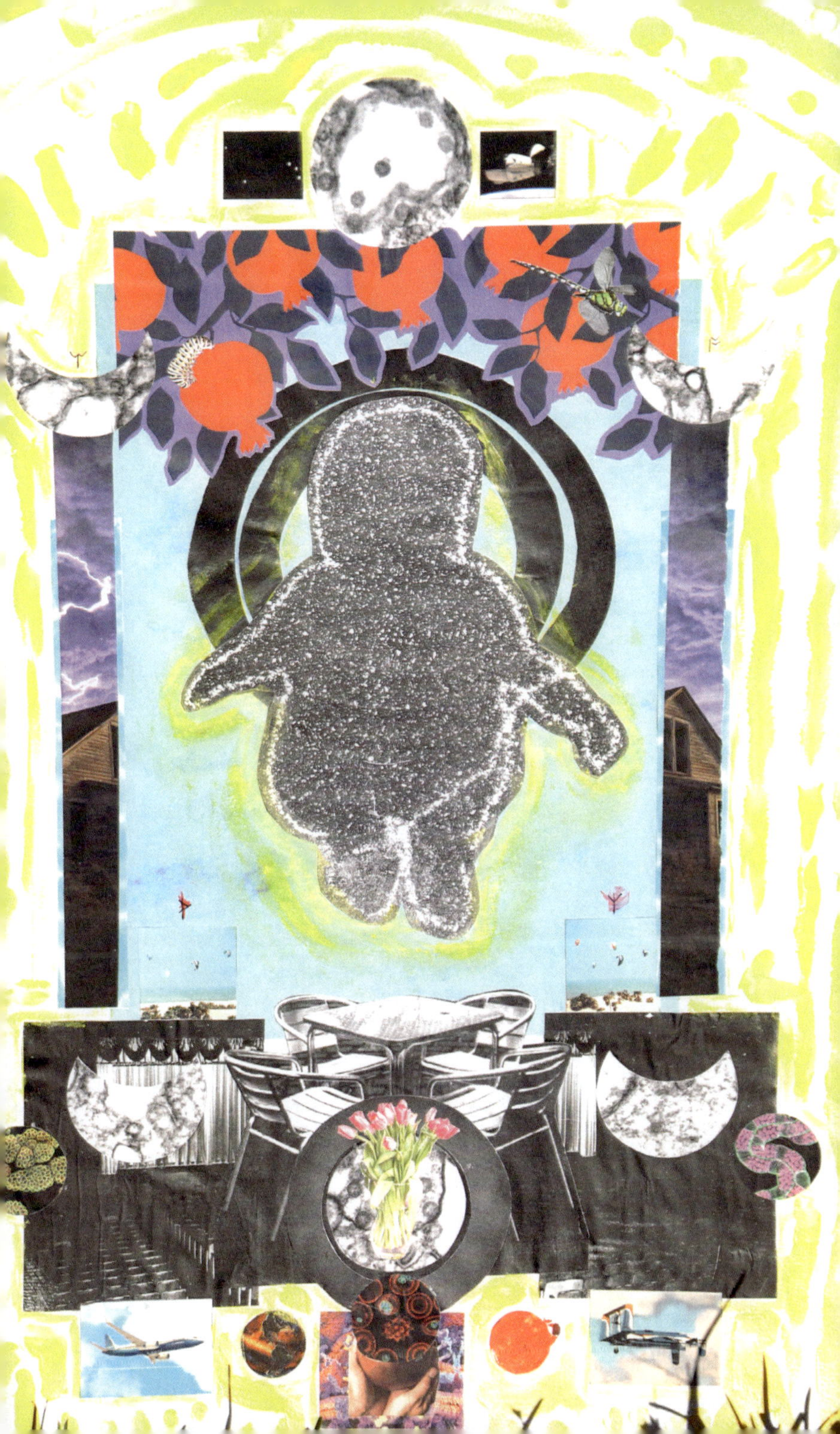

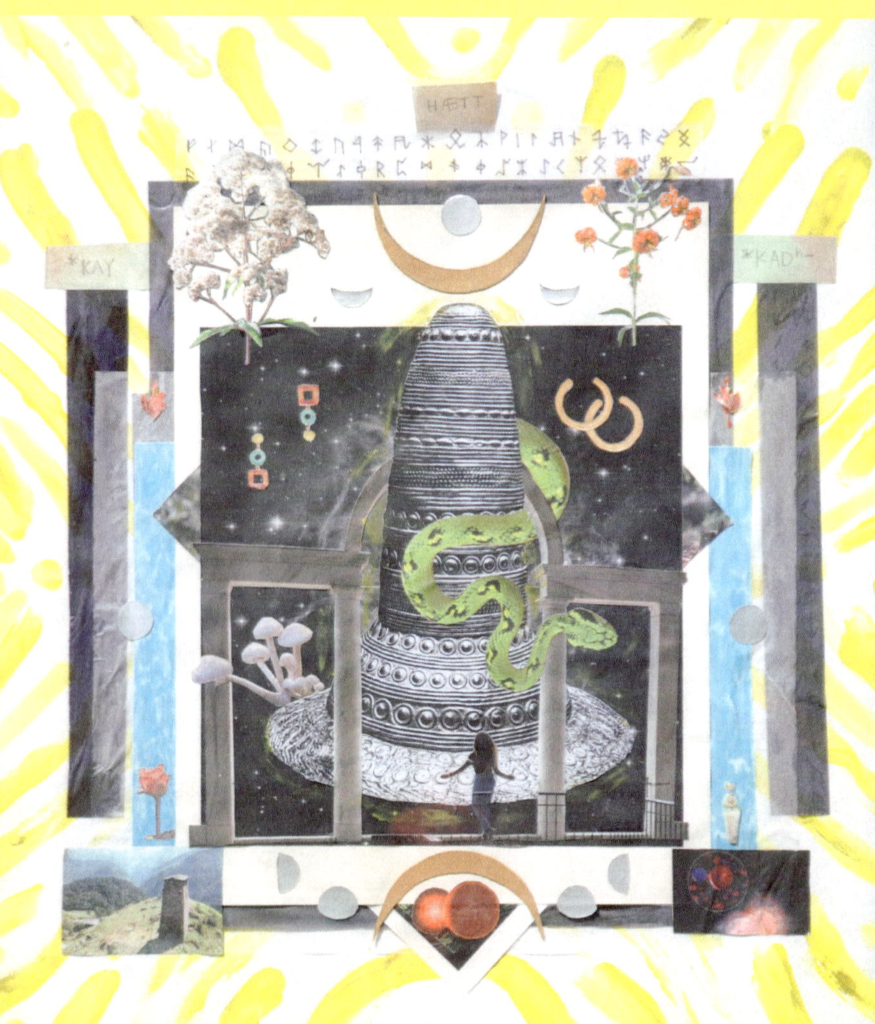
HÆTT
*KAY
*KADʰ-

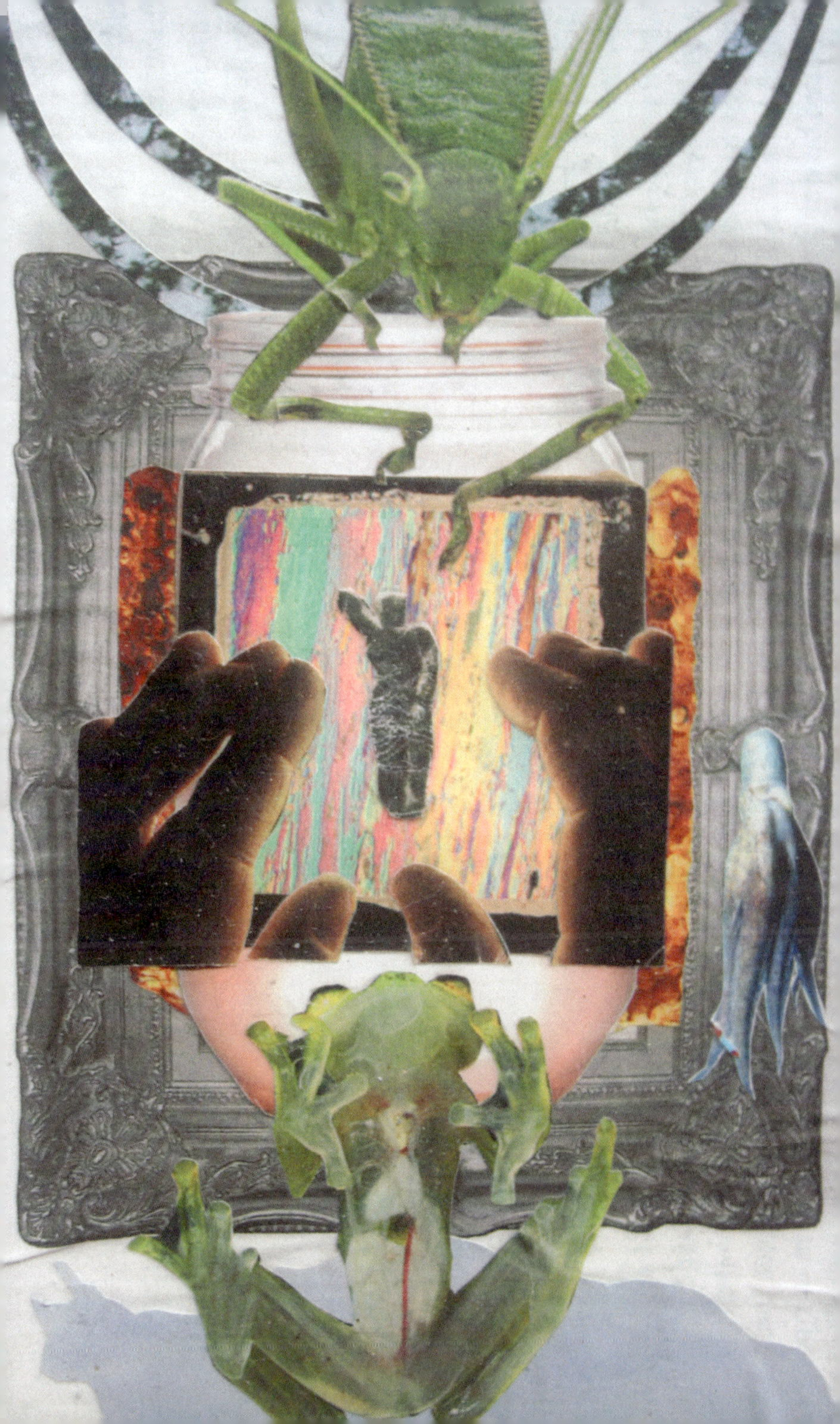

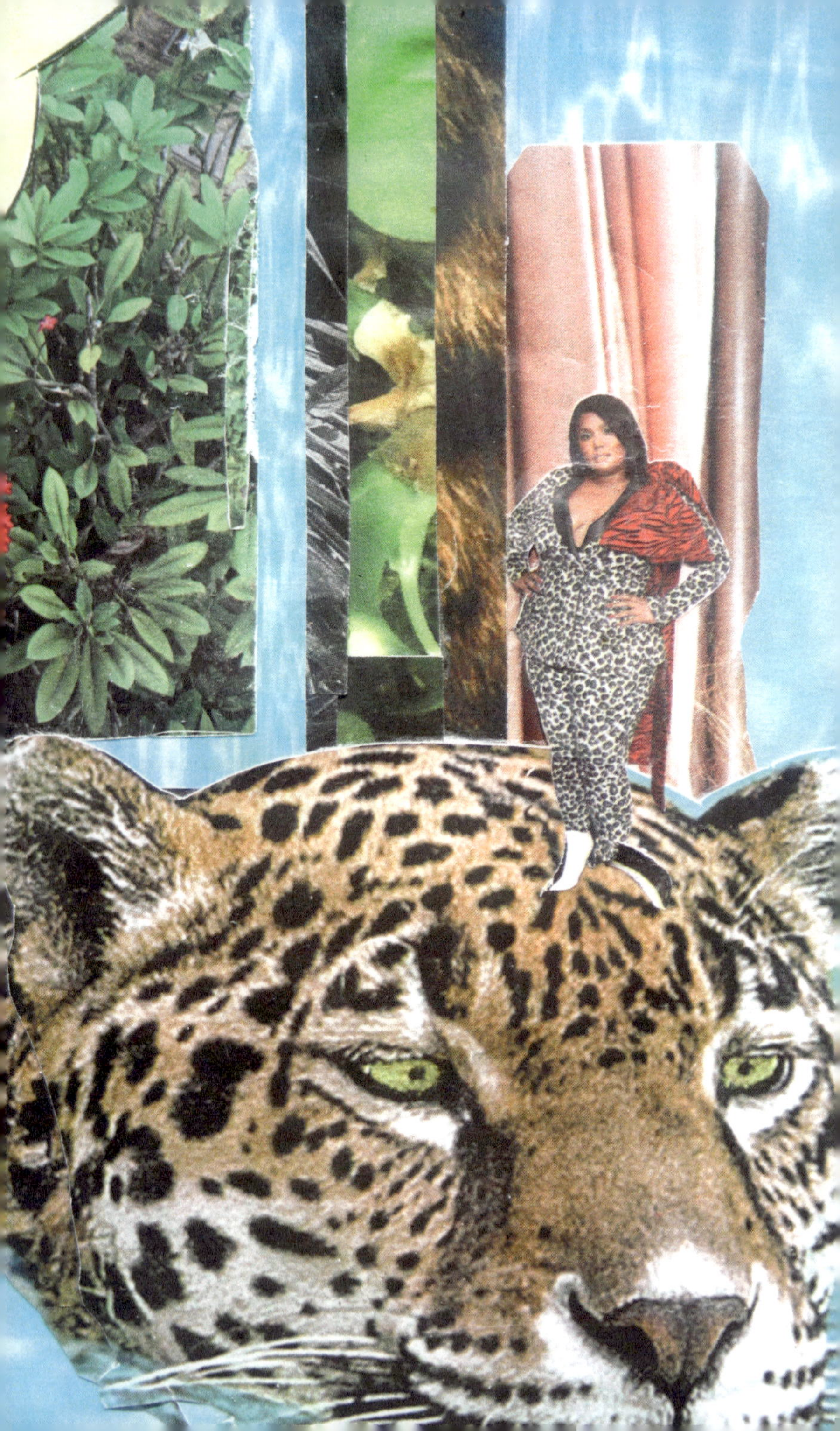

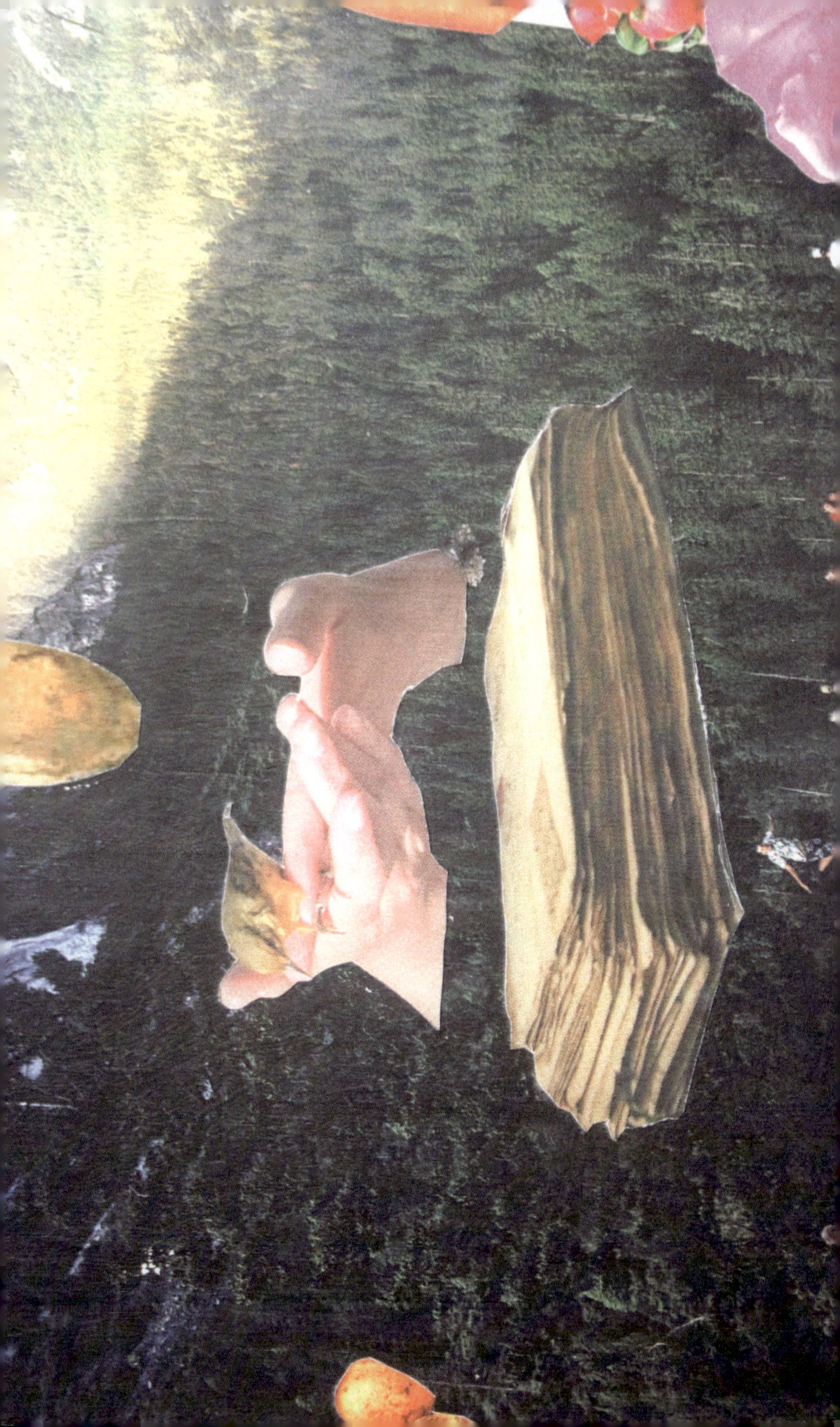

www.ingramcontent.com/pod-product-compliance
Lightning Source LLC
Chambersburg PA
CBRC090712070726
47599CB00031B/951